AUSTRALIA'S
GREAT BARRIER REEF

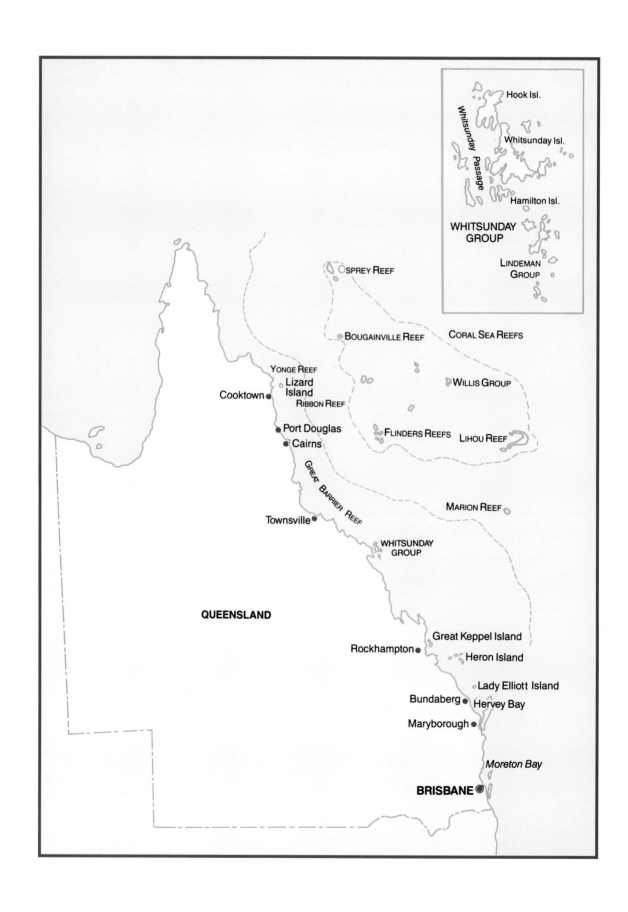

AUSTRALIA'S
GREAT BARRIER REEF

The pearly nautilus, Nautilus pompilius *(see page 39).*

NEVILLE COLEMAN

CHILD & ASSOCIATES
AN ALL-AUSTRALIAN PUBLISHER

Neville Coleman is a renowned underwater photographer and explorer. In 1969–73 he travelled 64 000 kilometres around Australia's coastline photographing, recording and collecting thousands of marine creatures. In 1984 he received the Commonwealth Medal for Advancement in Photographic Technology, the Australian Photographic Society's highest award.

Neville has written over thirty books and his articles have been carried, worldwide, by over one hundred publications. He is presently curator of the Australasian Marine Photographic Index, the largest visual identification system in the Southern Hemisphere.

Front cover, main photograph: *Reef scene.*
Front cover, inset: *The red hermit crab,* Dardanus megistos *(see page 32).*
Front endpaper: *Heron Island is a true sand cay built up over the ages from coral rubble, shell grit and coralline algae.*
Back endpaper: *These formations of staghorn coral,* Acropora *sp., are typical of the rich growths encountered around the Keppel Islands.*
Back cover: *The coral cod,* Cephalopholis miniatus *(see page 50).*
Below: *Angas' ovulid,* Phenacovolva angasi *(see page 22).*

Acknowledgements

All the photographs in this book were taken from the files of the Australasian Marine Photographic Index (AMPI). The Index contains colour transparencies of living animals and plants, cross-referenced against indentified specimens housed in museums and scientific institutions. It also covers related marine activities. The entire project is housed under the network of educational services offered by Neville Coleman's Sea Australia Resource Centre.

I would especially like to thank all the various curators and scientists at Australian museums and various institutes, the Great Barrier Reef Marine Park Authority, Queensland National Parks and Wildlife Service, Mr Jim Tobin of Oregon, USA, and Dr Walter Stark.

To the managements of Great Keppel Island Resort, Heron Island Resort and Lady Elliott Island Resort and all the various people who have helped through the many years it has taken to build the Australasian Marine Photographic Index Data Bank and make it one of the most significant of its kind in the world, many thanks.

Neville Coleman

Published by Child & Associates Publishing Pty Ltd,
5 Skyline Place, Frenchs Forest, NSW, Australia, 2086
Telephone (02) 975 1700, facsimile (02) 975 1711
A wholly owned Australian publishing company
This book has been edited, typeset and designed
in Australia by the Publisher
First edition 1990
© Neville Coleman 1990
Printed in Singapore by Kyodo-Shing Loong Printing
Industries Pte Ltd
Typesetting processed by Deblaere Typesetting Pty Ltd

National Library of Australia
Cataloguing-in-Publication data

Coleman, Neville
 Australia's Great Barrier Reef.

 Includes index.
 ISBN 0 86777 343 X.
 ISBN 0 86777 367 7 (limp).

 1. Coral reef flora—Queensland—Great Barrier Reef. 2. Coral reef fauna—Queensland—Great Barrier Reef. 3. Great Barrier Reef (Qld.)—Description and travel. I. Title.

919.43

CONTENTS

The Great Barrier Reef 8

Algae 18

Sponges 20

Cnidarians 22

Worms 28

Crustaceans 32

Molluscs 38

Echinoderms 44

Ascidians 48

Fishes 50

Reptiles 59

Mammals 60

Index 61

The Moorish idol, Zanclus cornutus, *is related to the surgeonfish but lacks the blades on the caudal peduncle.*

The Great Barrier Reef

Great Barrier Reef—three words which have echoed through the hearts and minds of millions. What is it about this huge wondrous structure that draws people to it from all over the world? Is it the multi-coloured tourist brochures with their dyed corals and barely clad damsels? Is it the air-conditioned ultra-modern units with four sumptuous meals a day and all the booze you can guzzle? Or is it the chance of seeing nature's largest creation in all its glory; to breathe the salty, untainted air and to revel at the clear night skies? It would be nice to think it was the latter, for the Great Barrier Reef is an adventure in itself, something in which all may share, from the youngest to the oldest—to sit on a white coral sand beach and watch as the receding tide eddies around the coral heads. Within minutes the surface is broken by one, ten, twenty and then countless hundreds of coral clumps which seemingly rise and break through the surface waters. Walking out into the shallows (adequately shod) and coming in close contact with these intricate structures is a beginning. But only a beginning, for although the calcareous architectures are beautiful they cannot compare with the fascinating animals which construct them.

The Coral Reef

The coral reef consists of communal groups of delicate, soft bodied polyps which combine salt water and their own body fluids to produce skeletons hard enough to pierce the hulls of a hundred ships. It is a throbbing magnitude of animals all living their lives in a predetermined pattern, a pattern which man is only on the threshold of understanding.

Opinion varies as to the age of the Reef. It is known that corals have lived in the area since Pre-Cambrian times, perhaps 4.5 million years. Some estimates suggest that the Great Barrier Reef has been in existence for 30 million years.

The most recent natural development has been controlled largely by fluctuations in sea-level over the past 600 000 years and the main phase of reef growth has taken place during the past 10 000 to 20 000 years.

A coral reef may be comprised of many hundreds of coral species, some similar in shape while others are singularly characteristic. They live for the greater part from mid-tide level down to, and a little beyond, 50 metres. Colonies may vary from several millimetres in size to massive monoliths 5 to 10 metres across. The low-tide fossicker sees only a minor fraction of these, for the majority live subtidally. It is the snorkeller or scuba diver who has the greatest opportunity to observe the true

The Great Barrier Reef is the greatest construction ever created by living organisms. The best way to appreciate its size and extent is to fly above it. (Wistari Reef—Capricorn Group off Gladstone.)

living reef. Most coral polyps are nocturnal and shun the light of day, but when the skies are overcast many feed during the daylight hours.

The majority of reef-building corals are colonial. Even though each polyp acts independently it is linked to its relations by common flesh. So, even though a coral clump may be a single object, it is made up of thousands of connected polyps all contributing to the colony as a whole. The food caught and eaten by each polyp helps to sustain the entire group. The general life history of the more common corals is well known throughout the world, and the Australian forms differ little from these.

Upon reaching maturity, coral polyps produce both sperm and eggs. At certain times of the year, when conditions are right (three to six nights after the full moon in December), the sperm and egg bundles are released into the surrounding water. Sometime later, after fertilisation has occurred, small gourd-shaped larvae emerge from the eggs and join the many millions of other minute organisms, called plankton, drifting along with the currents. Capable of some directive movement, motivation of the larvae is controlled by the backward and forward lashings of hair-like cilia which cover their external surface.

After several days to a week of drifting, the larvae settles to the bottom. The site chosen for settlement must be on hard, solid substrate and must be found within a short period of time otherwise the cycle is interrupted and the larvae will die. Anchoring itself with a glue-like secretion, the larvae gradually alters its shape to finally resemble a minute polyp. The polyp grows rapidly, lime begins to form in the tissues and a new coral colony is born.

Different types of corals form colonies in various ways. One of the most common methods of increasing the colony is by budding, this is where smaller corallites form at the sides of the larger ones, such as with staghorn corals. Another method is by division. Usually restricted to the larger brain corals, here the corallites split, forming separate polyps and as growth proceeds, separate corallites.

The colours of the stony reef-building corals are living colours and are only contained within the tissues of the polyps themselves. There is also another factor which adds to the colour of coral animals: imbedded in the polyps' flesh are thousands of minute single-celled marine plants called zooanthellae.

During the daylight hours these algae provide extra supplies of oxygen as well as absorbing some of the excess carbon dioxide given off by the polyps. At night, when corals feed, the polyps obtain oxygen directly from the water passing over, or through, the tissues.

Every type of coral is a carnivore and feeds mainly on large quantities of planktonic organisms which either drift or are directed towards the tentacles. Each tentacle is armed with batters of nematocyst pods. These pods resemble minute oval balloons filled with poison and contain a small coiled spring, tipped with a barbed dart. The instant a small animal brushes past the tentacle, it is

To put on a face mask and venture out into the shallows is like opening the window to a whole new world.

transfixed by hundreds of these poisonous darts. The tentacles then move the prey towards the mouth which enlarges and engulfs the animal. Digestion begins immediately and when the meal is finished the refuse is exuded from the mouth.

The corals contribute to the major bulk of building the Reef and could be referred to as the 'bricks'. However, another important life form provides the 'mortar' which binds and holds the bricks together, anchoring them against the forces of nature. This relatively insignificant looking group are the coralline algaes, of which many different species occur on the Great Barrier Reef. Often referred to as lithothamnians, these coralline algae are also able to extract calcium carbonate from sea water. They are found all over the Reef and are especially prevalent on the weather sides, where they form hard encrusting layers, holding and cementing the living and dead corals together to form protective ramparts against the tireless, erosive ocean.

9

Because of its warm climate and waters, the diversity of species and the numerous commercial aspects, there has been more marine scientific work carried out on the Great Barrier Reef than anywhere else in Australia. Yet the life histories of many marine animals remain a mystery, even today. Each year we learn more and more, yet it is what we do with what we learn that's important. Each person visiting the Great Barrier Reef has the potential to help.

The Great Barrier Reef Region

The Great Barrier Reef region is an area of approximately 350 000 square kilometres extending along the Queensland coast from the Torres Strait in the north to Bundaberg in the south. The Great Barrier Reef Marine Park, the largest marine park in the world, has been declared over most of this area. The Park contains more than 2500 reefs, banks and shoals. There are also over 900 continental and coral islands within its boundaries many of which are national parks. Many islands and coral cays support breeding colonies of migratory seabirds. Turtles, dugongs and whales also find refuge here. The fish, coral and other invertebrate communities represent one of the richest and

most diverse faunas in the world. Because of these special qualities the Great Barrier Reef has been inscribed on the World Heritage List.

The Queensland National Parks and Wildlife Service (QNPWS) is responsible for the day-to-day management of the Great Barrier Reef Marine Park on behalf of the Great Barrier Reef Marine Park Authority. The QNPWS also manages the island national parks and State marine parks in the Great Barrier Reef region. Co-operation between State and Commonwealth Governments is ensuring complementary management for these areas.

Management

The Marine Park staff develop educational programmes, run activities on reefs and islands and publish a variety of information for park users. A visitor centre has been established on Heron Island, a popular diving area. The centre provides educational material, and regular talks

Most environmentally concerned resorts feature educational reef walks. Excellent staff guides ensure that the often hidden features and their inhabitants become known to the visitor.

Underwater photography is really the only way to share and display the living treasures of the Great Barrier Reef. With so many excellent cameras available today, everybody from snorkeller to scuba diver can capture their own holiday adventures.

and slide shows are given for visitors. Marine Park rangers are stationed on the island.

Underwater trails have been installed at some popular diving sites such as Green Island and Lady Elliott Island reef. Lady Elliott Island is a favourite destination for local and overseas divers. Other trails are planned for Magnetic Island, Hook Island, Hardy Reef and John Brewer Reef.

Marine Park officers monitor the effects of recreational and commercial activities on reef and island ecosystems. Heavily used anchorages are identified and permanent moorings are installed to minimise damage to delicate corals. Inventories of seabird nesting colonies and island flora and fauna are being undertaken. This information is being used to develop management plans for many islands to ensure that the needs of visitors are balanced with the need for conservation. The QNPWS conducts underwater surveys and tagging programmes on coral trout in order to assess the effects of fishing on stocks of this prized table fish.

Several species of sea turtles are also the focus of a major research programme aimed at increasing our knowledge of these animals. Nesting female turtles can be seen on island beaches in the Capricornia and Far Northern Section of the Park from November to January.

The QNPWS also has a programme to develop and upgrade facilities for day visitors and campers on some islands. Facilities include picnic tables, freshwater tanks and toilets.

Regular aerial and boat surveillance provides information on user activities as well as a visible presence in the Park. Although emphasis is placed on the education of park users, Marine Park staff are empowered to enforce regulations when necessary.

How You Can Care For The Reef

Ultimately, the future of the Reef resides with the users. The Great Barrier Reef Marine Park consists of a number of sections and zoning plans have been prepared progressively for each section. These plans allow for reasonable use while also separating conflicting activities. The island national parks are fully protected. Currently, divers may visit most reefs and islands. Only those areas which are Preservation Zones, Scientific Zones or are seasonally closed to protect breeding wildlife are off-limits to divers.

Before visiting the area it is advisable to obtain a zoning plan for the Reef and visitor information for the national parks you wish to visit. Commercial spearfishing and spearfishing with scuba or hookah are strictly prohibited in the Park. Several groups of marine animals, plants and products are protected and may not be collected without a permit. Camping is allowed on many of the island national parks. However, as these islands are extremely popular with campers, you will need to apply for a camping permit well in advance (up to six months for some islands). For further information contact Queensland National Parks and Wildlife Service Head Office in Brisbane or their Regional Offices at Rockhampton, Townsville and Cairns.

The Great Barrier Reef Marine Park

The Great Barrier Reef region stretches over 2000 kilometres from its southermost point near Bundaberg to the northern tip of Cape York Peninsula. Over 98 per cent of the region is included in the largest marine park in the world, the Great Barrier Reef Marine Park.

The responsibility of management strategies has been vested in the Great Barrier Reef Marine Park Authority, a Commonwealth Government agency. The Authority's goal in the development and care of the Marine Park is to provide for the wise use, appreciation and enjoyment of the Great Barrier Reef in perpetuity.

Diving As An Activity Within The Marine Park

The Authority intends the area to be a multi-use park which provides opportunities for all reasonable uses, including diving, while still ensuring the long-term survival of the Reef.

The only diving-related activities totally prohibited are spearfishing with scuba and other underwater breathing equipment (except snorkel), the use of powerheads while spearfishing and the taking of Queensland groper and potato cods larger than 1.2 metres in length. Mining (except for approved scientific research purpose) and oil drilling are also prohibited.

Management Through Zoning

The main management tool used by the Authority is zoning. Zoning plans are designed to ensure a balance between human needs and the need to conserve the Great Barrier Reef, and to separate conflicting uses. They allow multi-use of the Reef's resources but restrict or prohibit certain activities in specified areas.

Zoning plans are in operation for all sections of the Marine Park. The plans are developed with the help of extensive public input so that the needs and the knowledge of people who use the Reef can be taken into account. The Authority also uses research data and information from various government and commercial agencies in developing zoning plans.

The Zones

General Use Zones The majority of the zoned part of the Marine Park is in one or other of the General Use Zones.

These allow all or almost all commercial uses. There is no restriction on diving or other recreational activities although collecting may require a permit in some of the General Use areas.

Marine National Park Zones Marine National Park Zones of various types are more like land-based national parks. They provide areas for recreational use such as diving. Limited fishing is allowed in some areas.

Special Zones Scientific Research Zones and Preservation Zones are small areas set aside from any normal use to preserve some areas of the Great Barrier Reef untouched.

Closure Areas Some areas may be closed for a period for a particular purpose. Seasonal Closure Areas protect some bird and turtle nesting sites during the breeding season while Replenishment Areas allow fish stocks to built up on some reefs. Reef Appreciation Areas set aside parts of popular reefs for diving and other peaceful enjoyment.

Zoning Plans Zoning plans and activity guides are available for zones sections of the Marine Park. Make sure you have copies for the areas you are visiting or travel with a reputable tour operator who is using a zoning plan. Zoning plans are obtainable from the Great Barrier Reef Marine Park Authority in Townsville, or from the office of the Queensland National Parks and Wildlife Service in the regional centres.

Park Management

The sheer size and complexity of the Marine Park means that management is also a task of immense size and complexity.

The QNPWS is responsible to the Authority for day-to-day management of the Marine Park. The management role of the QNPWS includes implementation of interpretive programmes, monitoring (for example effects of visitor activities), surveillance (by aircraft and patrol vessels), and enforcement. The QNPWS is also directly responsible for the management of the island national parks.

The major emphasis of management is on education. Increased awareness and understanding of the Marine Park will ensure that the users of the Marine Park, use and enjoy the Reef in ways which will conserve the beauty, diversity and abundance of life that makes the Great Barrier Reef such a magic world, particularly for divers who have the chance to experience this amazing underwater treasure at close quarters.

Further Information If you wish to find out more about the Great Barrier Reef Marine Park, particularly the areas in which you may wish to dive, please contact the Great Barrier Reef Marine Park Authority or the Queensland National Parks and Wildlife Service.

Visiting The Reef

The Great Barrier Reef is more than one reef, one island, one cay, or one bommie. It is many thousands of all these, each one different, each one with its own place, each one with its own special allure to diver, adventurer, naturalist, photographer or visitor.

To visit the emerald waters of nature's living architecture is the dream of almost every would-be, or could-be, holiday enthusiast. But 2000 kilometres of reefs and islands that stretch from Fraser Island in the south, to past the tip of Cape York in the north, is a formidable piece of territory from which to choose a once-a-year holiday destination.

Generally the best time to visit the Great Barrier Reef is during the dry season when the weather is more stable. This is between the months of June and December. The wet season with its thunderstorms usually begins around the end of December and lasts for three to five months. Some years are better than others but there are no guarantees. However, the weather makes little difference to the underwater inhabitants.

Birds are especially vulnerable to the increase in tourism. With more visitors and more encroachment on the birds' habitats even the regulations that now apply may not be sufficient in the future.

Conservation

With the growth in concern about environmental issues it has become increasingly obvious that Australians must change their attitudes towards the oceans and their inhabitants. We need to learn from the countries that have been exploiting their marine resources for thousands of years. The theory that 'the oceans will never run dry' is now proven to be entirely false.

Overfishing, short-sighted governments and the individual's greed have in many areas annihilated huge expanses of the ocean's produce to a point beyond recovery.

Australia is a fantastically rich country, but in the short space of two hundred years millions of hectares of semi-productive land have been destroyed by overstocking, elaborate deforestation and short-cut farming methods. Admittedly much of the damage was due to ignorance but we cannot allow such ignorance to destroy our oceans.

The degradation of the land can be seen quite easily by the naked eye, however we cannot see to measure our destruction and exploitation of the ocean. On land we can only harvest what crops can yield. In the sea we cannot know to what extent the total yield is, because we cannot see it. Estimations are only guesses based on inadequate information of probable stock numbers.

Pollution is a major issue. The sea is polluted by millions upon millions of litres of sewage, noxious poisons sprayed on crops eventually leach out into the rivers and end up in the sea, as do chemicals from factories, and detergents and chlorine from millions of households.

More extensive research and monitoring of our oceans and their resources is needed. Our scientific organisations are understaffed, underfinanced and underequipped. Only a handful of commercial marine species have been seriously researched. It will be many years before we even have recorded and can recognise all the animals and plants in our seas, let alone understand their complex inter-relationships.

There has been more research conducted on the Great Barrier Reef than any other area in Australia, yet even this

The era of the high-speed catamaran has heralded an unprecedented number of day trippers to the Reef: 10 000 to 15 000 visitors per day is estimated in the spring and summer seasons.

must be seen as small. Much of the knowledge about the Great Barrier Reef has been accumulated since the highly publicised upsurge in populations of crown-of-thorns sea stars.

Australia *can* successfully conserve its marine resources, all it needs is people who appreciate what we have, and who know that all we have to do to lose it … is nothing!

Clean Investment

Tourism is a stable, simply organised economic investment which is of high economic importance to the growth of Australia. Although there are many commercial enterprises which provide a higher turnover than tourism, many of these are subtractive processes which have an immediate or lasting effect upon the environment.

Many conservationists believe that by increasing the numbers of people visiting the Reef, significant problems may occur in regard to coral damage by fossickers. This opinion is not shared by others who maintain that as the majority of living coral and marine life is found below the low-tide level, the percentage broken by visitors walking on the Reef crest is too minimal to warrant consideration.

By means of subtle education programmes in brochures, advertisements and slide productions at the resorts, the delicate balance of the Reef and its inhabitants can be shared, along with the beauty. Some island resorts have already made determined inroads into informing visitors about the correct procedures necessary to share and yet preserve our greatest natural wonder.

Threats To The Reef

Without doubt the greatest single threat to the Reef itself is human. Without the necessary control over the greed of our own species we are liable to incur devastation in the sea similar to what has already occurred on the land.

Australia is far too young a country to plunge headlong into short-term profits in areas where our knowledge is microscopic.

Although there has been more marine research conducted on coral reef environments than on any other ocean area in Australia, we are only on the verge of understanding a few of the complex systems of this vast and unique natural wonder.

Crown-Of-Thorns

Undoubtedly the crown-of-thorns sea star has been the centre of the greatest controversy Australian marine life has ever known.

That this sea star's feeding habits led to large areas of living coral polyps being destroyed is on one hand to be regretted. On the other hand the search for a possible answer to the proclaimed wholesale destruction of the Reef led to the provision of more money for marine research than any other single factor.

Studies carried out have concluded what many suspected, than the upsurge in crown-of-thorns populations are a natural cyclic phenomenon which affects many species of terrestrial and aquatic animals from time to time. The reasons are still unknown, only the steady process of accumulating knowledge can possibly provide the answer to this one of nature's myriad secrets.

As far as the Great Barrier Reef being threatened with extinction by the crown-of-thorns sea star, there is little scientific evidence to support this idea.

Limestone Mining

The long-term effect of large-scale limestone mining of so-called 'dead reefs' would undoubtedly have implications far beyond the realisation of those other than biologists. There is no such thing as a 'dead reef'. Each square metre of dead surface coral often has hundreds even thousands of marine animals living in it. Fan worms, burrowing worms, molluscs, shrimps, crabs, fish, sea stars and sea urchins are all animals which in turn support the ecosystem and the food chains of larger predatory fish on which a great deal of the present Queensland catch depends.

Not only would huge masses of marine organisms be destroyed, but the water itself would be laden with tonnes of suspended sediment which would smother surrounding reefs containing live coral and have detrimental effects on all filter and suspension feeders.

Oil Drilling

Australia depends on supplies of oil for its power needs. However, to risk the destruction of such a unique and wondrous formation as the Great Barrier Reef is hardly in Australia's best interest.

The heavy cloud of industry has hovered over the Reef for many years. Only through the dedication, ability and hard work of avid conservationists has the Reef so far been saved from the short-sighted vandalism of big business and governments.

Even though oil companies have been thwarted for the time being they still hold many government granted leases and vigilance must be maintained by all Australians to see that our greatest natural wonder is preserved.

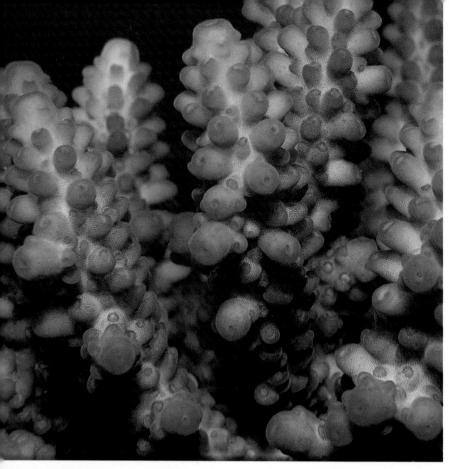

The colours in a coral reef can only be seen in their true magnificence when viewed close-up. Even in very clear water it doesn't take much distance for everything to blend into blues, greens and browns and then into grey. Yet each colony has its own colour, shape and pattern and when viewed close-up, even that which appears dull at a distance becomes beautiful.

The expanded polyps of the sunshine coral, *Tubastrea aurea*, are quite large (15 to 20 millimetres or more across) and dramatic in colour. Although this species is not a true reef-building coral in the same way as many others, it is without doubt one of the most beautiful examples of coral on the Great Barrier Reef.

Gorgonian sea fans display almost every colour of the rainbow. Their fragile connecting branches grow in genetically inspired patterns rimmed with delicate translucent polyps, beautiful yet deadly to their microscopic prey.

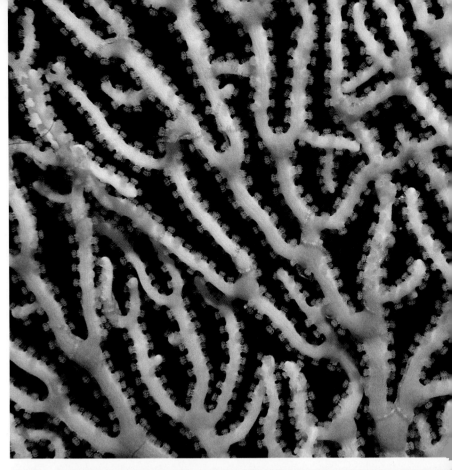

Although most people think of the Great Barrier Reef as animal dominant, it is really the plants which are dominant. As a light-dependent ecosystem the photosynthesisation of plants is the basis for all life on the Reef. Even the beautiful corals—animals themselves—derive 90 per cent of their total food and energy from microscopic algae called zooanthellae which live in their tissues and in many cases generate their colours. A living coral reef is really only a thin veneer, built, over thousands of years, on the skeletons of millions of its predecessors.

Algae

One of the numerous types of calcareous algaes found throughout the Reef, *Halimeda macroloba* grows from low-tide level down to 8 metres. It has a hard, multi-buttoned shape and, when alive, is deep dark green. A small commensal crab, *Huenia proteus*, may be found on this algae, its carapace being very similar in shape to the algae's leaf-like plates.

When *Halimeda* dies it breaks down to grit and powder. All species of calcareous seaweeds lend their bulk to building the Reef. This substance could almost be called the 'mortar' because by sifting into all the nooks and crannies it helps to bind and consolidate the Reef's structure.

Although quite common along the inner reef flat and in the sandy zone, grape weed, *Caulerpa racemosa*, is not always restricted to an intertidal habitat. A small, green, berry-like algae, it grows in dense mats in the lagoon and deeper pools. The berries are around 3 to 6 millimetres in diameter. Small green nudibranchs and bubble shells may be observed amongst its branches. This genus is fairly easy to recognise in its natural habitat but specific identification may need to be confirmed by an expert, as there are a number of different species.

Right

With its spectacular bright green tresses, turtle weed, *Chlorodesmis comosa*, is probably the most conspicuous of all the Reef algae. It appears out in the open in bright sunlight and many shallow lagoon coral clumps have 'head-dresses' of turtle weed. Tufts are generally around 76 millimetres in height and many clumps have the small commensal crab *Caphyra rotundifrons* and unidentified shrimps living among the waving fronds. On some reefs, growths may be seen down to depths of 20 metres but it is much more common in shallow areas.

18

Sponges

Common in the deeper waters of the Reef, the spectacular yellow fan sponge, *Ianthella flabelliformis*, has a skeleton of thick fibre which can actually be seen through the thin tissues. The skeleton holds the colony erect, though the surface is quite soft to touch. This species grows to a height of around 500 millimetres and is generally seen growing in positions facing into the prevailing currents. The inhalant pores are on the front of the sponge and the larger exhalant pores, on the back. In some specimens the colour towards the base may be pink.

Virtually unknown to most Australians, and extraordinary in its artistic visual design, the red medusa sponge is an encrusting species which is often found on the undersides of loose stones, dead coral slabs and the walls of caves. Most colonies are small in size, being only patches up to 100 millimetres across, though some cave-dwelling colonies may spread over a metre or more.

The red medusa sponge is different in function from many other sponges, its inhalant pores are in the red tissue and when water passes through and the food and oxygen content are filtered out, the wastes are exhaled by the overlaying white canals.

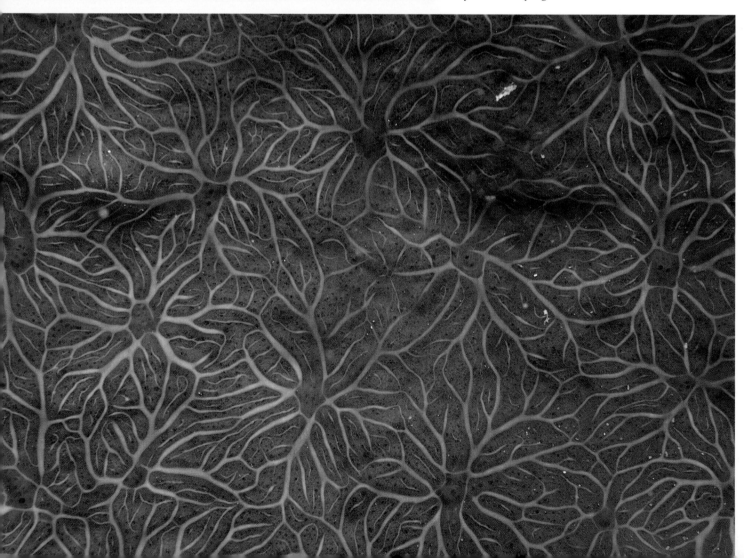

The volcano sponge, *Pericharax heteroaphis*, is a moderately common subtidal species, which grows to a height of around 300 millimetres. Colonies can be seen on reef slopes and attached to coral heads from 10 to 20 metres. The volcano sponge generally has fluted sides and is often streaked with yellow. This sponge is relatively brittle to touch and has triradiate spicules capable of penetrating human skin. The only predator observed on this sponge is Gardiner's notodoris, *Notodoris gardineri*, a sponge-eating nudibranch.

Cnidarians

With feeding tentacles extended during the daylight hours, as well as at night, shield coral, *Turbinarea peltata*, is able to catch microscopic plankton upon which it feeds at twice the rate of its competitors, which may account for its fairly speedy growth rate. Similar to all corals, its flesh and tentacles contain minute stinging cells called nematocysts which kill or immobilise its drifting, or settling, prey, these are then transferred to the mouth

Corals of the genus *Turbinarea* are able to exist in far more temperate waters than the majority of tropical corals and extend right down the coast to offshore central New South Wales.

A resident predator on many colonies of gorgonian sea fans is Angas' ovulid, *Phenacovolva angasi*, an exquisite little allied cowry which feeds on gorgonian tissues. The mantle of the ovulid is almost exactly the same colouration and pattern as the sea fan. It lives on one specific sea fan for its entire life and its mantle polyps often mimic the extended feeding polyps of that sea fan.

Angas' ovulid grows to around 25 millimetres with the female growing larger than the male. Mating takes place in spring to summer and the female attaches her eggs to the branches of the sea fan.

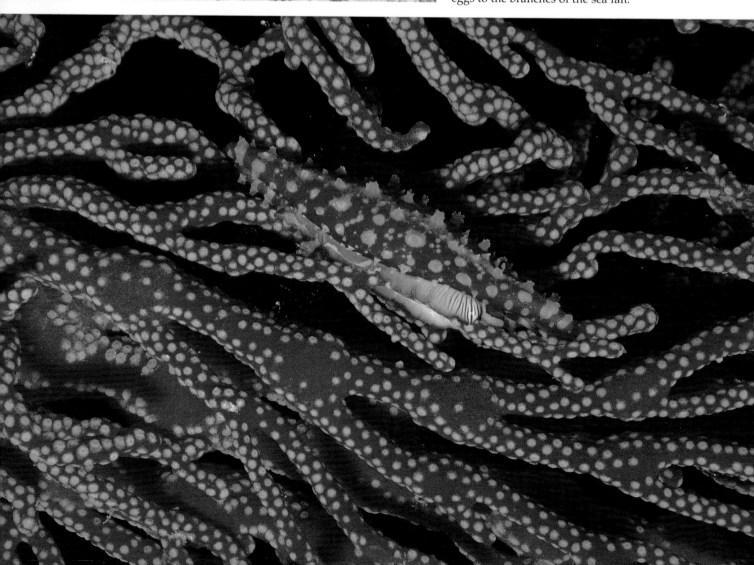

Named for its visual similarities in pattern and shape to the exposed brain of a mammal, the term 'brain coral' covers several different genera within the class Anthozoa. One of the most massive brain corals is *Leptoria phrygia*, the embroidered brain coral. Unlike other brain corals, the septa of the embroidered brain coral is quite ordered, though it has the most meandering pattern of all corals. It is present in both inshore and offshore waters and it extends all along the Great Barrier Reef. It ranges in colour from greens to browns and grey. Not all colonies are as perfectly rounded in shape as the one illustrated here.

Generally observed in deeper waters, around 30 metres, the strange soft coral sea fan, *Siphonogorgia* sp., grows in small isolated clumps on rocky outcrops on the sides of bommies. Unlike many other gorgonian sea fans this species has no central wire-like skeletal core and has only unarticulated spicules within its tissues.

The structure is quite brittle and branches will break off very easily. Similar to other alcyonarians its polyps have eight pinnate tentacles and these may be extended both day and night.

Colonies grow to around 300 millimetres in height and the species appears to be restricted to the northern extent of the Great Barrier Reef around the inshore islands and reefs.

The spiky soft corals, *Dendronephthya* sp., are the most spectacular of all subtidal soft corals. The colonies are usually found in areas of strong tidal influence along channel bottoms or adjacent reef slopes. They stand erect by pumping themselves full of water which is displaced through interconnecting vessels within their tissues. The spikes are sharp and will penetrate soft skin but cause no other detrimental effect. In some areas, deep water specimens may reach a height of over 1.5 metres. Associated animals observed on spiky soft coral include spider crabs, porcelain crabs, shrimps, brittle stars, ovulid molluscs and nudibranchs.

It is sometimes difficult to separate the white stinging sea fern, *Lytocarpus philippinus* (pictured below), and its relative *L. phoeniceus* in the field. However, *L. philippinus* tends to live in shallow water and is mostly brilliant white, whereas *L. phoeniceus* may be greyer. One thing is certain, for anyone stung by either of these hydroid colonies the correct identification becomes the furthest thing from mind. The sting is instantaneous and if on an unprotected, sensitive part of the body, can be very painful. Post-injury reactions may also be severe, taking the form of unbearable itching that may last up to three weeks.

The only predators observed to feed on this species are the masked angelfish, *Chaetodontoplus personifer*, and a predacious nudibranch.

Sunshine coral, *Tubastrea aurea*, is restricted to a subtidal habitat and is generally observed at a depth range of from 3 to 30 metres. It grows in small round clumps and although the polyps can be seen extended on overcast days, it is during the hours of darkness that their stunning beauty is seen at its best. Colonies occur beneath overhangs, in caves, or on the sides of coral heads where current, or wave action, is moderate.

A small nudibranch, *Phestilla melanobranchia*, is a specific predator on sunshine coral, feeding both on polyps and tissue. The filaments on the nudibranch's back are almost identical with the retracted polyps of the coral, making it almost impossible to detect. The golden wentletrap, *Epitonium* sp., is also a significant predator on sunshine coral.

The elegant hydrocoral, *Stylaster elegans*, is found growing inside caves and under ledges on coral reef dropoffs along the outer barrier reef and throughout the Coral Sea. Small clumps (up to 100 millimetres in height) may be seen inhabiting dark caves and ledges in waters as shallow as 5 metres all along the Great Barrier Reef.

In southern New South Wales it has been recorded from 120 metres. The elegant hydrocoral is extremely fragile and is often inhabited by a small predacious mollusc allied to the cowry family, *Pediculariona stylasteris*. Barnacles also infest the living colonies, particularly the shallow-water forms.

Because the identification of Australia's living soft corals is not complete, this fairly prolific group remains relatively unknown in the field. However, the widespread tropical genus *Dendronephthya* can be identified in the field by experienced observers.

The spiky soft coral occurs in a multitude of colours—orange, red, pink, yellow, white and mauve—and generally inhabits areas of moderate water movement, such as the sides and bottoms of reef channels or drop-offs. Its stem colour is usually a translucent 'ground glass' pink.

The clumps of coloured spines in the vicinity of the polyps are very sharp and serve a similar purpose as thorns on a rose bush, to protect against predators.

Among the most common types of reef-building, shallow-water corals, the staghorns are represented by almost fifty species. Some species can be identified in the field, but most can only be determined by an expert.

The pictured form is found on shallow reefs to 10 metres. Staghorn corals are extremely variable in shape and form and in many cases their environment controls the eventual shape of the colony. The polyps of *Acropora* corals appear from individual corallites which are ranged along the sides of the main branch.

Parrotfish often feed on living staghorn corals, as does the crown-of-thorns sea star, *Acanthaster planci*.

With an appearance reminiscent of nothing on earth, the leathery-like exterior mass of Trochel's soft coral, *Sarcophyton trocheliophorum*, at low tide with all its polyps retracted is hardly likely to be considered an animal by the majority of uninitiated reef walkers. However, animal it is, in fact a whole colony, all living in unison. When submerged by the incoming tide the polyps emerge from within the firm gelatinous tissue and feed on the rich planktonic 'soup' brought in by the rising waters. Although the soft corals have similarly structured polyps to the hard corals, they differ by having eight tentacles, which are always pinnate—similar to a feather with processes along each side.

Sea fans are also referred to as gorgonians, a common name derived from their scientific order, Gorgonacea. The red and white sea fan, *Melithaea* sp., is fairly common and is regularly observed from 5 to 30 metres. Usually found in areas of strong tidal influence, the colonies generally grow on the sides of coral heads and along channel slopes and bottoms. The red sea fan, *Melithaea* sp., may reach 2 metres in height and the structure always faces at right angles to the current flow, allowing the polyps to derive maximum planktonic food intake from the water. Feather stars often use this species as a feeding platform and the ovulid molluscs, *Pellasimnia semperi* and *Phenacovola* sp., are resident predators.

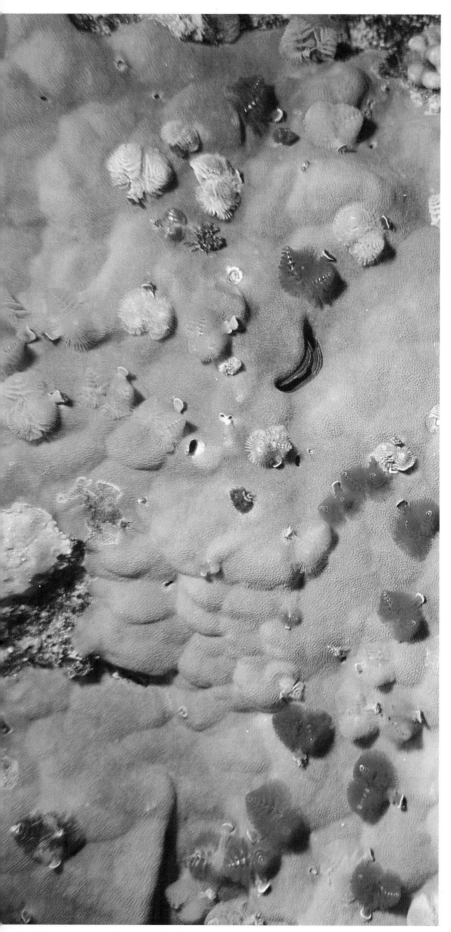

Worms

Left and below

Exhibiting every colour of the rainbow, the tropical feather duster worm, *Spirobranchus giganteus*, would pose an identification problem if the species was determined on colour alone. However, for several reasons it is readily identifiable in the field.

The feather duster worm almost always builds its calcareous tubes in the living colonies of corals and hydrocorals. It is especially prevalent in large coral 'heads' with small polyps, such as *Porites* corals. Sometimes as many as fifty worms will be found in one square metre of coral head. The delicate, twin, spiralling radioles are cone-shaped and the operculum has two minor extensions on the lower edge.

Spirobranchus giganteus is the only species of the genus so far recorded in Australia and other coral-inhabiting tube worms are easily distinguished by the shape and size of their radioles.

With its bright white and red feeding and breathing radioles extending some 100 millimetres out into the current from its tube entrance, the giant tube worm, *Protula* sp., is an impressive sight. Not as common as some of its smaller relatives, the giant tube worm generally inhabits depths of from 3 to 25 metres where its calcareous tube is found buried in coral rubble or located between clumps of dead coral rock. It has fairly stable colouration throughout its range and feeds both day and night on plankton and suspended sediment which is trapped in its feathery gill-like plumes.

Above

Throughout its distribution the liparis flatworm, *Pseudoceros liparis*, is subject to colour variation ranging from pure white to bright blue. However, the black median lines down the centre of the animal's back and the red peak behind the front palps generally remain standard.

This worm is far more commonly encountered at the southern end of the Great Barrier Reef, especially in the Capricorn Group. It grows to 30 millimetres and is active both day and night. Quite often juveniles of this species may be seen together and at times they may feed on the same food source.

Growing to over 120 millimetres, Hancock's flatworm, *Pseudoceros hancockanus*, is one of the largest flatworms in the Reef waters. It is an active swimmer. Like the Spanish dancer nudibranch its reaction to danger is to swim up into the water column by flailing itself backwards and forwards. This has often caused it to be mistaken for that particular mollusc. Hancock's flatworm is active in the open during the day and due to its protective chemical deterrent is not harmed by fish. Many flatworms have similar protection and though some may be attacked by inexperienced juvenile fishes, they can repair any damage by regeneration.

Feeding on compound ascidians (colonial sea squirts) the coral flatworm, *Pseudoceros corallophilus*, is a roving diurnal forager that inhabits both inshore and offshore reefs. Its colours are fairly stable and it grows to around 28 millimetres. The knowledge of flatworm natural history and identification are still very limited on Australian species with some thirty or forty species still awaiting scientific description. The majority of flatworms are far more simple to identify from a colour transparency or print (once they are identified from a preserved specimen and cross-referenced) than from a preserved specimen alone. They lose their colour and pattern, and in some cases disintegrate, when preserved.

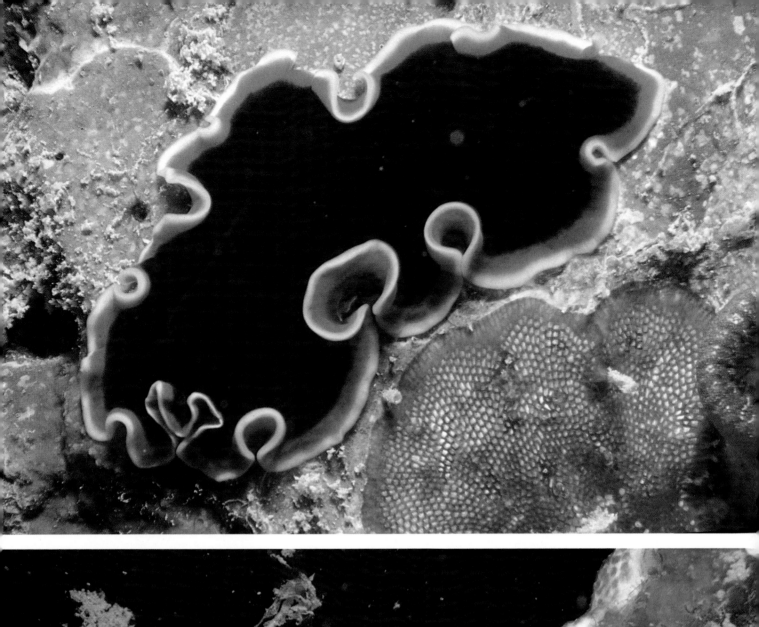

Crustaceans

The largest of the Reef hermits, the red hermit crab, *Dardanus megistos*, grows in excess of 250 millimetres and can be found from low tide down to 30 metres. During the hot sunny days it seeks the shelter of cool reef recesses beneath coral or under rocks. Mainly predatory, red hermit crabs also scavenge and are able to derive nourishment from detrital feeding. Although many species of smaller hermit crabs are gregarious, the adult red hermit crab lives as a solitary. Hermit crabs have no protective exoskeletons for their soft parts; to survive they must utilise the shells of dead molluscs, changing to larger ones as they grow.

Rarely seen out on the Reef during the day, Hiatt's hinge-beak shrimp, *Rhynchocinetes hiatti*, is one of the most spectacular members of the nocturnal fauna. Generally observed in a solitary situation, specimens grow to around 80 millimetres and have the longest rostrum of any of Australia's hinge-beak shrimps. Although there have been some reports of commensal relationships between some hinge-beak shrimps and sea urchins, this does not appear to be more than a loose association.

The shrimp hide behind the sea urchins during the day when the urchins inhabit the same ledges.

The splendid reef crab, *Etisus splendidus*, spends its days hidden in dark labyrinths of coral and rocky reefs. Solitary in its habits, the crab ventures forth at dusk to the undersides of ledges and holes in the Reef, in search of the algae upon which it feeds.

During the hours of twilight the splendid reef crab is never fully exposed and is very sensitive to movement. However, at night when there is no moon, it will venture into the open to feed. This crab is fairly slow in its movements but is extremely powerful and clings tenaciously to the substrate when caught; in fact, to remove the crab one must demolish the substrate first. The splendid reef crab should on no account be eaten, as it is very poisonous.

Living in an endoetic (sheltered or protected) relationship with several species of sea anemones, the spotted procellanid crab, *Petrolisthes maculatus*, is pictured here on an anemone host.

When this species of anemone crab is found on isolated anemones there are often two crabs in residence, a male and a female. However, when there are many anemones in close proximity to one another, only one crab may be present. Although the anemones that shelter these little crabs are capable of stinging, killing and eating much larger crustaceans, the spotted procellanid crab scuttles among the stinging tentacles and may even enter the mouth and stomach without being eaten.

The feeding mechanism of this crab comprises two modified appendages (maxillipeds) which are among the mouthparts. These long arm-like appendages are thickly fringed with long pinnate hairs. They are flung out and returned in a alternate rhythmic procedure, catching plankton and suspended sediment, which are filtered out. The food is then transferred to the stomach.

The depressed gorgonia crab, *Xenocarcinus depressus*, is easily identified in the field by its red colour and opaque white stripe down the back which does not vary throughout its distribution range. Restricted to a specific habitat among the fronds and branches of tropical gorgonians, these brightly coloured little crabs are usually found in pairs. There seems to be a difference in the size of adult crabs, depending on whether they are found on the west coast or the east coast. Adults from the Great Barrier Reef tend to be larger than those observed from northern Western Australia.

Some gorgonian fans may have dozens of small juvenile crabs clinging to their fronds. Most of these young ones either succumb to predators, or move on to other gorgonians as they grow. Observations on small gorgonian clumps show no large adult aggregations.

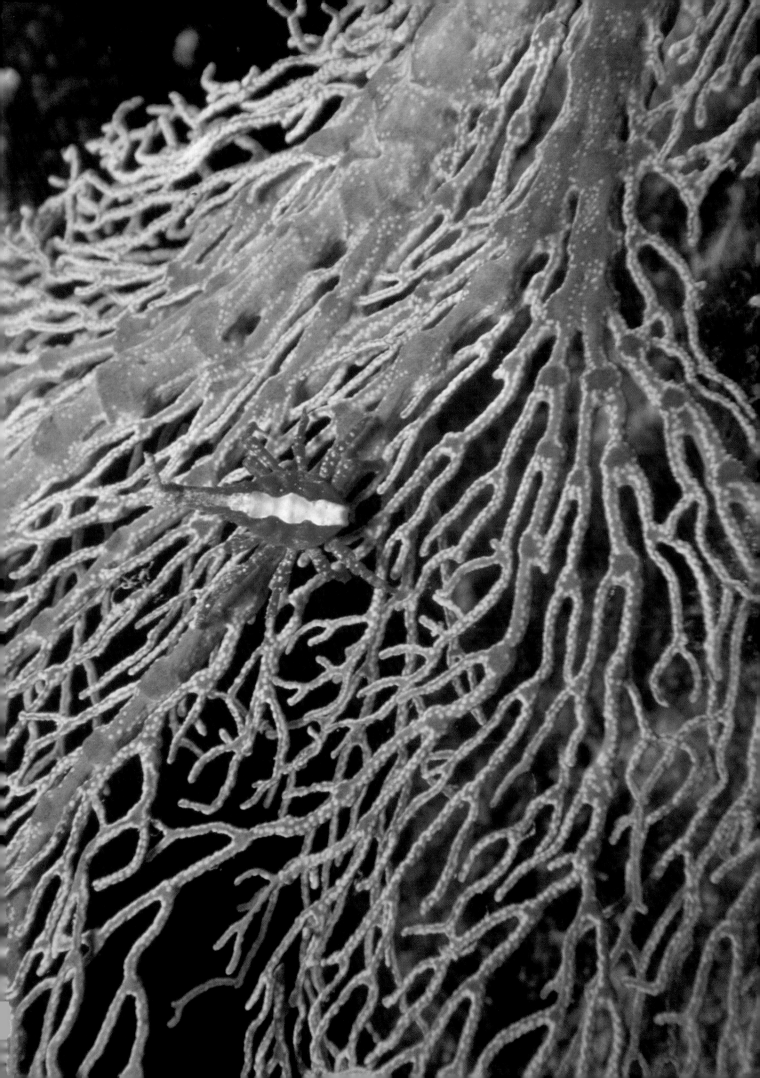

The banded coral shrimp, *Stenopus hispidus*, inhabits the Pacific and Indian oceans and is without doubt the most well-known and thoroughly researched species of all cleaner shrimps. Easily recognised by its long white antennae, red and white striped body, and chelae, the banded coral shrimp generally occurs in pairs or a group of pairs.

Adult males and females are similar in size and, once they have paired, inhabit the same station for several years. During the breeding season the female carries a clutch of green eggs beneath her abdomen.

Cleaning stations are generally in coral or rock crevices, in caves or under ledges. Although this shrimp is active during the day, much of its cleaning activity is performed on sleeping fish during the hours of darkness.

Cutting and picking functions are performed by the pincers of the secondary legs. The large chelae are used only for display or threat behaviour.

Most people are aware of the little snapping shrimps which inhabit the undersides of stones, or burrow tunnels in the mudflats where at low tide their sharp staccato can be heard echoing out over the tidal flats. The noise comes from their extra large nipper which has a spring-hinged pincer with a nodule which slams into a socket in the lower pincer. This large nipper is used for noise making and also for defence. Relatives of the snapping shrimp have found other ways to defend themselves. Stimpson's snapping shrimp, *Synalpheus stimpsoni*, (pictured) is commensal on feather stars where it spends its entire life hidden away amongst the protective arms of its host.

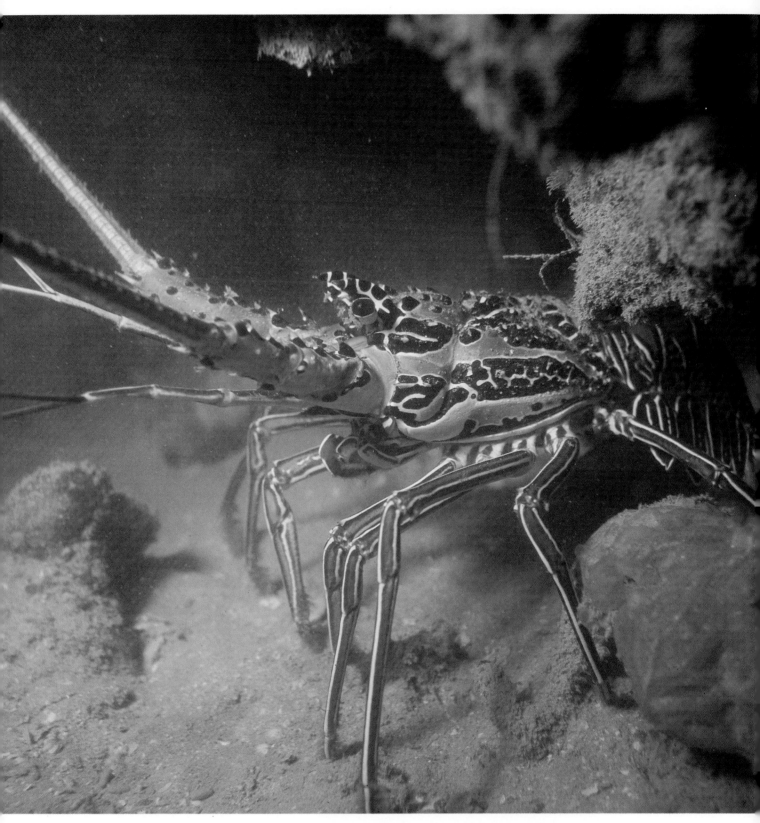

The largest and most spectacularly coloured tropical cray, the painted cray, *Panulirus versicolor*, inhabits the more sheltered aspects of coral reefs and lagoons throughout the Reef. Although specimens have been located in deeper waters, beyond 25 metres, most are observed in depths from 3 to 10 metres. Young crays may be seen living in small groups, but large adults tend to be solitary in their habits. Painted crays do not readily enter traps or pots and in the past this has led fisherman to believe they are vegetarian. However, this species is a carnivorous predator feeding on molluscs and, as with other members of its family, it also scavenges on dead or dying animals.

Molluscs

Without doubt the most well known of all the Australian baler shells is *Melo amphora*. It is very common on the intertidal mudflats of Queensland and Western Australia and is also trawled in deep water off the continental slope. Between these two extremes and in almost every habitat this baler shell is a sought after commercial species.

One of the largest univalves in the world, the extended animal from a large shell may measure up to one metre in length. The sexes are separate and, in general, the females are larger than the males. Mating takes place during winter months and eggs are laid at the beginning of summer in translucent honeycomb masses which harden into a tough plastic-like substance on contact with air or sea water. After laying, the female deserts her eggs, which hatch a month or so later.

Baler shells feed upon other molluscs. Both bivalves and univalves are consumed, including sea hares. Once the prey is captured, the baler envelopes the smaller shell into a pocket at the rear of its foot and then burrows beneath the sand. By a process of suffocation, the prey becomes flaccid and is consumed by the baler, after which the empty shell is discarded.

An active diurnal herbivore, the ass's ear, *Haliotis asinina*, is one of the largest tropical haliotids and can be seen intertidally on coral reef platforms in lagoons just on the turn of a flooding tide. During this time it comes out of hiding to feed. When the incoming tide covers the reef *Haliotis asinina* must once again hide away from predatory fish.

The animal and mantle of the ass's ear are far larger than the shell and for this reason the shell is protected from the ravages of sea and encrusting organisms and is always smooth and shiny. The sexes are separate, and eggs and sperm are released into the water where, when fertilised, the eggs form into larvae and drift with the plankton before settling on the bottom.

Living in the respiratory tract on the gills of some specimens is a small commensal pea crab, *Pinnotheres* sp. This crab has only been noted on a few occasions and its biology is relatively unknown.

When alive, the pearly nautilus, *Nautilus pompilius*, resembles an octopus but is beautifully striped and has many more arms. Unlike the paper nautilus, whose shell is actually the female's egg case, the pearly nautilus is attached to its shell by a siphonal tube which extends through a small central hole in the coils. The chambers in the nautilus shell are filled with gas and by means of this tube it can adjust the amount of gas in each chamber allowing the mollusc to rise or sink at will. Mostly a deep-water dweller, it bumps along the bottom in depths below 200 metres yet migrates vertically up into shallow waters at night to hunt for food. It feeds on crabs and other invertebrates and is caught and trapped off the Great Barrier Reef.

The tiger cowry, *Cypraea tigris*, is the largest cowry on the Great Barrier Reef. It generally occurs in intertidal lagoons, in caves, on coral clumps, and beneath underhangs of reef ramparts. Each cowry varies in colour pattern and size, the largest, up to 120 millimetres, are found at the southern extremities of their range. It is basically a nocturnal forager, but specimens can be seen also in the late afternoon on a flooding tide, feeding on encrusting algae on top of micro-atolls in lagoons. Long tactile papillae stud the mantle and these usually have an opaque white spot on the tip.

This species is often gregarious. Little is known about its breeding habits, but egg masses have been observed beneath coral slabs, with the female sitting on the eggs. Small crustaceans are sometimes present on the mantle but no definite association has been proven.

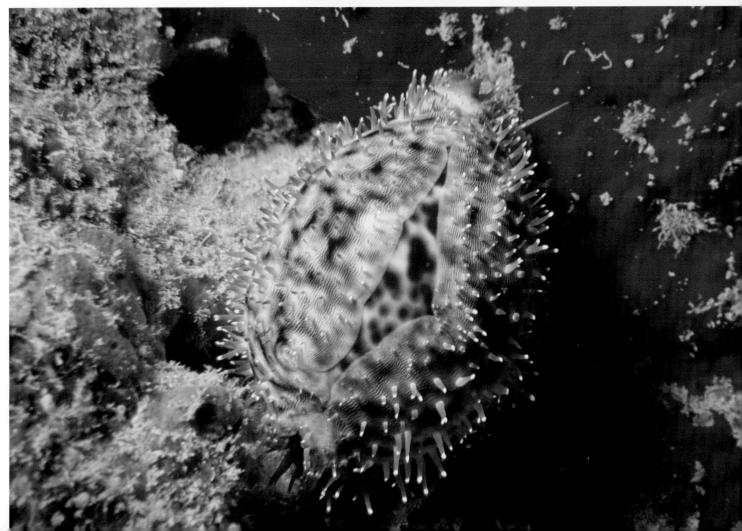

The map cowry, *Cypraea mappa*, is one of the most beautiful of Australia's larger tropical cowry shells. It is sparsely distributed on the Great Barrier Reef. It seems to seek areas of good aeration below the low-tide level and lives in caves and holes in the roofs of reef-edge overhangs where there is maximum water movement.

The map cowry's diet consists of sedentary encrusting organisms which it feeds on mainly during the hours of darkness. This is a protective measure to ensure minimum exposure to predation by fish. Wrasses are particularly fond of cowries; large fish crush the shell to get at the animal and smaller ones bite off chunks from the tentacles, mantle and foot. The mantle of the map cowry is a translucent buff colour with very few papillae. Under natural conditions it is not extended during the day.

Easily recognised in the field by its size and the characteristic sculpture of leaf-like flutes, the giant fluted clam, *Tridacna squamosa*, displays very beautiful mantle lobes. It is a filter feeder and lives below tide level in the shallow waters of coral reefs. Specimens can be found on sand or in coral to depths of 10 metres. It grows to around 400 millimetres and is fairly common throughout the length of the Great Barrier Reef.

The Heron Island volute, *Cymbiolacca pulchra*, grows to 100 millimetres and inhabits sandy rubble areas from low tide down to 3 metres. It is a carnivorous mollusc and feeds copiously on other molluscs, especially bivalves and univalves.

In the late afternoon, at dusk or at night on the rising tide it usually comes out of the sand in search of food. Once captured, the prey is held within the foot of the animal and taken below the sand to be eaten.

Very little is known about the breeding or egg-laying habits of this species. Its predators include baler shells, fish and hermit crabs.

Ovula ovum is the largest species of allied cowry found in Australia. Although the molluscs belonging to the family Ovulidae are similar to true cowries in internal features, the shells are somewhat different. As a family, the allied cowries have one common link—they feed on particular types of soft corals (alcyonarians). On the north-eastern coast of Australia this species is normally very abundant and is usually found in the vicinity of Trochel's soft coral, *Sarcophyton trocheliophorum*. Sometimes as many a five or six molluscs can be observed feeding on the same colony of soft coral.

The stark white of the shell and black colour of the mantle of the egg cowry facilitates finding and identification of this mollusc. Occasionally specimens can be seen moving across open sand or rubble patches. These are either seeking new feeding grounds or looking for a mate. Males tend to be smaller than females.

The egg capsules are clear and contain round blobs of white eggs. These are attached in clusters to the underside of the soft coral host.

Easily recognised by its unusual tent-like markings, the textile cone, *Conus textile*, lives in several different habitats. During the day it seeks hiding places beneath rocks or coral and generally buries into sand under these objects.

A nocturnal hunter, the textile cone feeds almost exclusively on other univalve molluscs. By homing in on expired waste products drifting through the water, this cone tracks down a prey species and usually chooses molluscs which have no operculum. When close to the prey species, the textile cone expands its long proboscis and tentatively explores the other shell. Having found the aperture the proboscis enters, probing into the depths. Upon contact with the flesh, a modified radular dart is shot into the prey, which succumbs to the cone's venom. Later the dead animal becomes flaccid and is consumed by the cone.

Textile cone poison is capable of harming humans and several victims are reported to have died through being stung by this species.

The toe-nail cowry, *Calpurnus verrucosus*, is an easily recognised allied cowry which seems to restrict its choice of food to the soft coral, *Lobophytum pauciflorum*. On large colonies of this soft coral there may be as many as six molluscs. They are mostly found in pairs and during the day seek shelter beneath the folds and 'fronds' of their prey.

The peculiar callouses on the anterior and posterior dorsal extremities of this shell are often tinged with mauve and it is from these unique growths that the mollusc gets its common name.

The toe-nail cowry feeds mostly at night, although it can sometimes be seen walking on the surface of its host during a flooding tide in the late afternoon or when the skies are overcast. Males are often smaller than females and mating takes place in the spring. In early summer the female lays her egg capsules on the soft coral host. The egg capsules are circular and rather flattish, and contain yellow-green eggs that tend to blend in with the soft coral upon which they are laid. The egg capsules may be laid directly on to the side of an overhanging 'finger' of soft coral or else may be laid on the underside of a flap, along the edge of the column. The female usually stays close to the eggs but does not sit on them, as do the true cowries.

The Spanish dancer, *Hexabranchus sanguineus*, which grows to about 300 millimetres, is the largest commonly encountered nudibranch species living on the Great Barrier Reef, where it can be observed in a number of different habitats, from low-tide level down to 20 metres. As with most nudibranchs, the Spanish dancer has no shell for protection; its survival depends on glands which produce an acidic chemical substance unpalatable to most other forms of marine life.

Specimens found in some lagoons are often inhabited by the beautiful little imperial shrimp, *Periclimenes imperator*, which is often a resident commensal.

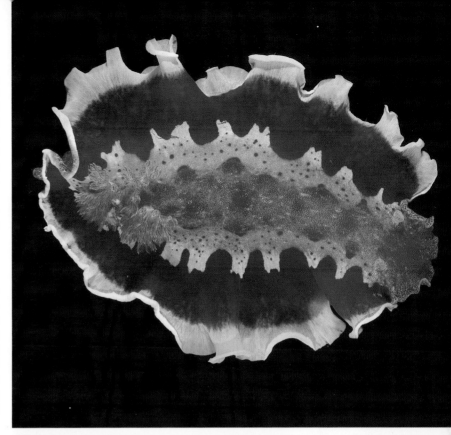

A very distinctive nudibranch which ranges throughout the Reef, Elizabeth's chromodoris, *Chromodoris elizabethi*, grows to around 40 millimetres and inhabits areas from low-tide level down to 25 metres. Similar to most chromodorids, it is a sponge feeder, grazing mostly on encrusting sponges of undetermined species. Diurnal in its lifestyle, Elizabeth's chromodoris is an open range nudibranch found on reef walls, in gullies, and along the sides of chasms and caves. It isn't found beneath boulders or rocks during the daylight hours.

Echinoderms

The large, conspicuous noble feather star, *Comanthina nobilis*, occurs along the Great Barrier Reef and has two main colour forms. One is as pictured and the other is dark green and black with yellow markings. The noble feather star may have over a hundred arms and thousands of sticky pinnules which, if touched, cling to hands, wet suit, and camera.

Most specimens observed are generally in an inverted position in the open, clinging to a piece of reef. Posture is maintained by the arms, as the cirri are small and almost degenerate. When disturbed, this species tends to form into a ball and roll with the swell or current until it lodges against an object. The arms once again begin to move in slow alternate rhythm, moving the feather star until it finds a favourable position. Hidden deep within the enveloping arms around the central disc lives the white commensal shrimp, *Synalpheus stimpsoni*. This shrimp generally occurs in pairs.

One of the largest, more easily recognised holothurians, the variegated sea cucumber, *Stichopus variegatus*, lives on a sand or rubble bottom from low-tide level down to 30 metres. It feeds by passing sand and coral detritus through its intestines to extract nourishment from the organic matter clinging to the grains.

The variegated sea cucumber often hosts the slim-bodied pearl fish, *Carapus* sp., which takes refuge in the sea cucumber's body during daylight hours. The imperial shrimp, *Periclimenes imperator,* may also reside on the body surface of the variegated sea cucumber in a commensal relationship.

Extremely common in lagoons and coral pools along the Great Barrier Reef, the spiny sea urchin, *Diadema setosum*, is a conspicuous and easily identified species. The main distinguishing factor between this urchin and its nearest Australian relative *D. savignyi* is the orange or light-coloured ring around the anal cone at the centre of the animal's upper surface. This feature remains constant throughout the urchin's geographical range and is also stable in juvenile stages. Fully adult specimens are an intense velvety black in colour with five prominent, iridescent blue and white markings running vertically down the test from the anus.

Juveniles and sub-adults have striped spines. This species is generally gregarious and during daylight hours often forms into groups, sheltering along the shady sides of coral pools, beneath ledges and coral. At night the groups disperse over the sea floor to feed on algae and detritus. The spines are venomous.

Rarely seen in its natural habitat, this delicate little star with its well-defined shape and colour pattern, offers no problems in regard to its identity. The icon sea star, *Iconaster longimanus*, is the only representative of its genus in Australia. Although this species is common in dredgings, little has been recorded of its natural history.

It is known to live on rubble bottoms, in channels between reefs, on reef slopes, and under coral slabs. It has been recorded in the Capricorn Group on the Great Barrier Reef and in the Whitsunday Group.

The crown-of-thorns sea star, *Acanthaster planci*, is the only venomous sea star recorded in Australia and it should be avoided at all times as its spines are capable of causing severe injuries. It is interesting to note that twenty-five years ago this rather unusual sea star was regarded as uncommon. Since then the number of observations has increased steadily and in many isolated areas of the Great Barrier Reef large populations have been sighted.

In some respects it is regrettable that this sea star's feeding habits have been responsible for the depletion of many hectares of living coral. However, despite the negative predictions, the Great Barrier Reef is not in danger of being devoured in its entirety by this animal.

The small shrimp *Periclimenes soror* has a commensal relationship with some crown-of-thorns sea stars. Known predators include the pufferfish, *Arothron hystrix,* and the giant triton, *Charonia tritonis,* but there is little evidence that these animals are more than opportunist predators.

Although the crown-of-thorns ate vast areas of coral reef while it was present in plague proportions, it is this very fact which led scientists, government bodies, business interests and the public to donate huge amounts of time and money to investigate the many factors surrounding the phenomenon. Knowledge of corals, sea stars, molluscs, fish, etc., has been gained many years ahead of what would otherwise have been possible.

The elusive sea urchin, *Asthenosoma intermedium*, was first discovered on a reef off Lindeman Island on the Great Barrier Reef by the late naturalist Melbourne Ward who contributed so much to our early knowledge of Australian crustaceans and echinoderms. Since then, intermittent sightings have been recorded at Houtman Abrolhos, Western Australia, off Townsville, Queensland, and at Wistari Reef in the Capricorn Group.

It is a large sea urchin which inhabits coral and rocky reef slopes and isolated coral outcrops in channels and between patch reefs. It blends into its habitat so well that it is often hard to distinguish. Its spines produce an extremely painful sting and this may be another reason why the animal has been ignored.

Two main colour forms have been observed, one predominantly red and the other yellow. This urchin is sensitive to disturbance and in comparison with other large tropical urchins, can move along the bottom at remarkable speed. Its food is algae and detritus scraped from the surface of dead coral. The elusive sea urchin is the only known host to Coleman's commensal shrimp, *Periclimenes colemani.*

The princely sea star, *Pentaceraster regulus*, has several brilliant colour forms, which tends to make identification a little confusing. However, as this species only occurs on sandy, muddy or light rubble bottom around the coast and inshore Great Barrier Reef islands, the field is narrowed somewhat. There is only one other representative of this genus in Australia.

The princely sea star feeds by extruding its stomach and absorbing organic matter lying on the sand or mud surfaces. This process generally begins during the period of the incoming tide. Two commensal relationships have been noted with this species, involving the shrimp *Zenopontia noverca* and the small portunid crab, *Lissocarcinus polybiodes*.

It is very difficult to imagine a better known or more distinctly hued species than the blue sea star, *Linckia laevigata*. The stark blue colouring is rarely found in other sea stars, yet it is not always a good criterion for identification as this star may also be grey, pink or yellow when observed at different localities throughout its distribution.

Growing to more than 300 millimetres, the blue sea star generally inhabits pools or submerged reef flats in the vicinity of the reef ramparts. Its habitat on the Great Barrier Reef itself seems to be restricted to the reef flats and reef edge. It is not often seen below 5 metres. It may have several resident copepod commensals and, on occasion, a commensal flatworm.

Ascidians

One of the most attractive of the smaller communal ascidians, the distorted ascidian, *Pyctnoclavella detorta*, is more common than most people realise but, due to its small size, it is often overlooked. Growing to 35 millimetres, each stalk is attached to the main body clump which in some cases may only be 50 millimetres across. The colony grows by budding, a process of asexual reproductive growth.

Occasionally several clumps may be found together, but in general they are not very gregarious. Colours vary little and as yet no predators have been recorded.

Reaching a size of around 195 millimetres the golden ascidian, *Polycarpa aurata*, is a solitary ascidian which is more prevalent in the northern reaches of the Great Barrier Reef waters. Its bright purple markings and golden background colour make it easy to identify visually and on many inshore reefs it is very common.

Solitary ascidians are often referred to as tunicates and as such they have two body openings: the larger, which is generally lower down the body, is the inhalant opening and the smaller, is the exhalant opening.

Moseley's ascidian, *Didemnum moseleyi*, is an interesting species of colonial, encrusting ascidian which grows in investing sheets over many surfaces. It is not confined to Australian waters but ranges into many areas of the Indian and Pacific oceans. The species seems to be variable in colour as it has been recorded by Kott as being yellow-orange.

The colour form illustrated is from the Capricorn Group on the Great Barrier Reef and in this area the colour ranges from deep purple to light mauve, with white rims around the openings. Fairly firm to the touch, *D. moseleyi* has a beautiful lattice-like outer skin.

The only collected purple-blue colour forms of the sea star, *Bunaster variegatus*, have been taken from beneath or around encrustations of this ascidian. Normally *B. variegatus* is brown in colour.

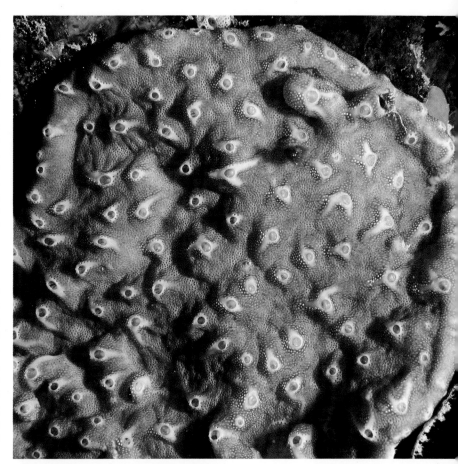

For many years during the early times of underwater exploration divers thought these attractive, very common little communal ascidians were sponges because they only had one exhalant siphon. The secret of the soft didemnum, *Didemnum molle*, is now common knowledge and has been published on numerous occasions. These delicate little colonies grow to around 25 millimetres and are generally found grouped together. The green colour within is the result of the animals being inhabited by masses of minute blue-green algae which grows as a symbiont in the ascidians' cloacal cavity. The outside colouring can be white, brown or greenish.

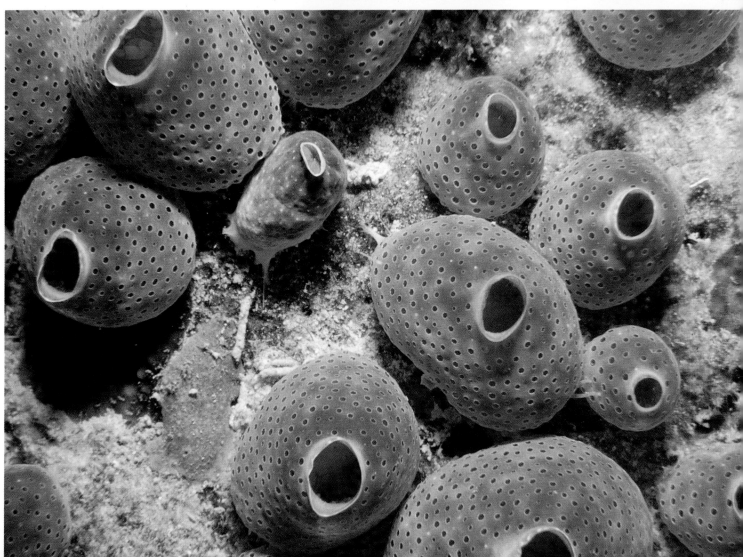

Fishes

The coral cod, *Cephalopholis miniatus*, is a true reef fish as it rarely leaves the caves, ledges, holes or labyrinths within its territory to swim in the open. It is one of the most brilliantly coloured of its family and throughout its range the red base colour seems to be consistent. The uninitiated may often confuse the common coral trout, *Plectropoma leopardus*, with this species. However, the slightly concave head, larger blue spots over the entire body and the convex posterior tail margin all combine for easy identification.

The coral cod is active during the day and feeds mostly during the hours of early morning and towards dusk. It grows to 45 centimetres and its diet consists of other reef fish and crustaceans.

The blue-lined surgeonfish, *Acanthurus lineatus*, is a fast swimming surgeonfish which can be seen on continental island reefs where there is moderate current, or water movement, around headlands and on seaward platforms and reef rims.

One of the most beautiful of all the surgeonfish and one of the most common, this species lives on and around the tops of reefs where it maintains a small area of algae-covered reef usually adjacent to territories of other of its kind.

Although attractively coloured, the fish must not be handled with bare hands while still alive as it has razor sharp extendable blades on the caudal peduncle which can inflict deep wounds.

For many years the horrid stonefish, *Synanceia horrida*, was thought to occur only on and around the muddy reefs of mainland estuaries, bays, inlets and lagoons and the fringing reefs of mainland islands off northern Australia.

Since this species was photographed at Tryon Island on the Great Barrier Reef in 1969 these facts have been updated. As our knowledge increases it is inevitable that there will be many changes to records, now and in the future. The horrid stonefish is one of the most venomous fishes in Australian waters. Concealed in dorsal sheaths along the back, are thirteen of the most efficient natural injection systems to be found in any marine animal. Needle-sharp spines, each with a twin venom sack, produce wounds of unbearable pain and a human victim must receive medical attention as soon as possible. Far more common than most people imagine, the horrid stonefish owes its success to camouflage techniques, for when buried in the substrate it is almost impossible to distinguish from its surroundings. It grows to about 33 centimetres long.

A large family of tropical butterfly and coralfishes, the chaetodons are the most distinctively marked, colourful and well known of all reef fishes. One of the most attractive species, the beaked coralfish, *Chelmon rostratus*, inhabits areas of broken coral and reefs in both sheltered and exposed conditions. Although juveniles may be seen on the reef flats, adults generally live in deeper waters. Adults are observed mostly in pairs, but solitary fish are not uncommon, and 'family' groups of adults with juveniles are also seen. The beaked coralfish feeds during the day, using its long tube-like mouth to pick small invertebrates and organisms from the reef.

At night it sleeps in holes and often wedges itself into the roof crevices of underwater caves.

Without doubt the best known cleaner fish, the common cleaner wrasse, *Labroides dimidiatus,* has entertained and educated thousands of divers, naturalists, photographers and aquarists for many years. These little fish (they are generally in pairs) set up what is known as a cleaning station. This is a common cleaner wrasse's territory to which all other fish in the immediate vicinity come to be cleaned of ectoparasites that cling to their skin, fins, mouth and gills. It is extremely important for a fish to go to a cleaning station regularly otherwise it becomes infested with parasites and is more likely to succumb to predators.

Rarely observed out in the open during daylight hours, the blue-stripe squirrelfish, *Sargocentron tiere,* is a species only recently recorded on the Great Barrier Reef. Very shy in its nature, this species is a nocturnal predator which comes out from its caves and ledges after dark to prey on small nocturnal crustaceans. It grows to 34 centimetres and can be distinguished from other squirrelfishes by the pattern and colour of its dorsal fin.

The orange-banded coralfish, *Coradion chrysozonus*, is fairly easy to approach underwater and is easily maintained in aquaria.

These little fishes seem to prefer deeper waters around back reefs and coral bommies where they spend the day picking at invertebrates in the marine growth on cave walls and around the bases of coral clumps. On occasion, pairs have been observed to range over an area of 30 to 40 metres. They also occur on broken bottom in moderately deep water. At night, orange-banded coralfishes sleep in crevices in the coral caves.

Seldom encountered by line fisherman, the black-spotted pufferfish, *Arothron nigropunctatus*, is sometimes taken in trawls and is regularly seen by divers. The dorsal colouring may vary between brown and grey. The black spots and the black patch around the anus are stable features, as are the black mask around the eyes, black mouth and black base on the pectorals and dorsal fin. Like all pufferfish, this one has the ability to blow itself up with air or water when it feels threatened. On no account should this fish to be eaten as it is deadly poisonous.

This exquisitely coloured four-lined snapper, *Lutjanus kasmira*, inhabits inshore reefs, continental islands and the Great Barrier Reef. It is commonly seen in the open around coral heads where there are large caves and gutters. The four-lined snapper is sometimes difficult to approach underwater. Juveniles form medium-sized schools but most adults swim in small groups, rarely alone. Throughout their wide distribution they do not appear in large numbers at any one location and seem to prefer depths below 20 metres.

Certainly the most common and best known in its genus, the fire fish, *Pterois volitans*, is the favourite of all underwater photographers and many aquarists. It occupies territories on mainland and offshore reefs and in some areas is quite common.

Mostly found in shallow waters the fire fish has venomous dorsal spines (as do all scorpionfish) and grows to a size of 38 centimetres. Its body colour ranges from pink to black and it is crossed with thin pairs of white bands. An easy method by which to separate the species of the genus *Pterois* is to look closely at the pectoral fins, each one has characteristic shape regardless of the colours or geographical location.

The emperor angelfish, *Pomacanthus imperator*, inhabits reef areas along the Great Barrier Reef and around a few of the more northern continental islands. Rarely seen in pairs except in the mating season, solitary fish are very territorial and are often observed in caves and grottoes on the edges of slopes, gutters and surge channel overhangs. Similar to many of the larger angelfish, the juveniles are quite different in colouration to the adults. Emperor angelfish juveniles are dark blue with white markings forming a circle on the back of the body.

Because of its excellent edible qualities, the red emperor, *Lutjanus sebae*, is a well-known reef fish with adults reaching a weight of a little over 20 kilograms. The sub-adult form, as pictured here, tends to inhabit shallower reef areas than adults, usually around 20 to 40 metres. The red emperor is also known as the government bream because of the similarity of the red bars on its sides to the early convict government 'arrowhead' sign.

It generally feeds during twilight and at night, consuming molluscs, crustaceans and fish. Sometimes juveniles accompany small schools of other bottom feeding fishes.

The adult fish are bronze red with white edges to their fins and a white stripe on the tail.

Unlikely to be mistaken for any other species, the painted flutemouth, *Aulostoma chinensis,* has three main colour phases: bright yellow, grey with white markings and red with white and black markings. This fish inhabits shallow waters around inshore and offshore reefs where it is an efficient diurnal hunter. Very often this species chooses another fish to hide its approach when stalking schools of small damsels or other fishes upon which it preys. The cover fish are either herbivores or large carnivores that only hunt at dawn or dusk. By choosing this type of cover the painted flutemouth is able to sneak-attack unsuspecting prey. Yellow phase flute-mouths normally choose yellow cover fish, whilst grey phase forms choose dark cover fishes.

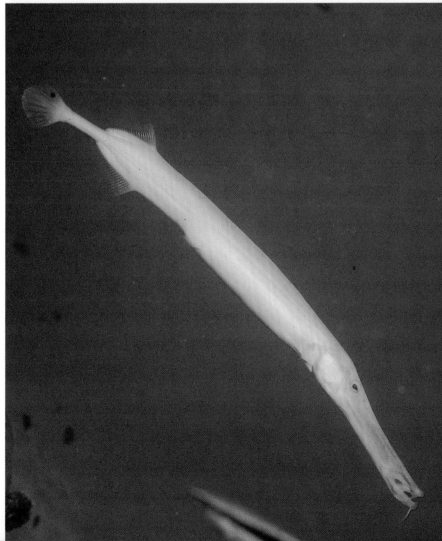

55

There is little doubt that wrasses are among the most beautiful of fish. They are also one of the largest families, the most difficult to identify (because of their many colour phases) and very difficult to photograph. The yellow-green wrasse, *Thalassoma lutescens,* inhabits inshore and offshore reefs and islands along the Great Barrier Reef where it is quite common in some areas. The common name was originally derived from the female which has a yellow head and green body. Similar to most wrasses this species is sexually dichromatic. The males reach a size of 30 centimetres and are not as numerous as females.

Found on inshore and offshore reefs throughout northern Australia, the white-tipped reef shark, *Triaenodon obesus,* is a slender-bodied inquisitive shark growing to 2–3 metres.

Although it has formidable teeth and may be a little pugnacious during feeding frenzies or in the presence of speared fish, it is generally fairly placid and doesn't trouble divers unduly. It will take hooked fish from lines but isn't quite as much trouble as the gray reef shark.

Unlike many pelagic sharks, this shark does not need to swim continuously to keep water flowing over its gills. The white-tipped reef shark rests on the bottom using muscular gill movement for breathing.

The hussar frequents inshore and offshore reefs along the Queensland mainland and out onto the Great Barrier Reef.

The hussar, *Lutjanus ladetii,* forms large schools during the day, sheltering in large caves, or beneath ledges, often in the vicinity of a cleaner fish station. The hussar is a very attractive little snapper, with its bright pink colouration and yellow median stripe, making it easy to identify. They are very common in the Capricorn Group at the southern end of the Reef. At Heron Island the fish are so numerous and tame and often come so close to divers that it is impossible to get far enough away to take good photographs.

The manta ray, *Manta alfredi,* grows to 5.75 metres and may be seen from just below the surface down to about 30 metres. They feed on zooplankton which is sieved from the water through their mouthparts.

The young are born alive and come out of the mother's body wrapped up in the wingflaps. These unfold and the pup may measure 1 metre across at birth.

Snorkelling with one manta ray is an experience, but to be in the water in close proximity to several of these harmless giants, who on occasion allow humans to ride them, is one of the most exhilarating and exciting encounters imaginable.

When in waters that have not been frequented by humans, the Queensland groper, *Ephinephelus lanceolatus*, is inquisitive and home ranging. It will investigate almost any intrusion into its territory and may often become pugnacious and downright offensive until the object of its displeasure is removed or goes on its way.

Although much as been written about the predatory instincts of giant gropers no serious unprovoked attacks against humans are known to have occurred in Australian waters.

Adult Queensland gropers grow to 3 metres and are mostly solitary around offshore reefs but tend to become gregarious when in the vicinity of wharves and wrecks in the green coastal waters. Their diet includes mud crabs, turtles, fish crays and offal which are sucked into gaping jaws as the cod creates a vacuum by opening its huge mouth close to the prey.

Reptiles

The olive sea snake, *Aipysurus laevis*, is without doubt the most common species of sea snake encountered by divers in the waters of tropical Australia. Colour varies from brown to yellow. Although it grows to 2 metres and is highly venomous, its so-called aggressive behaviour is due mainly to its poor eyesight, curiosity and attraction to movement.

The olive sea snake is active both day and night and moves around on the ocean floor investigating crannies beneath coral and rocks in its search for food which is usually small demersal fishes. Several different species of fishes are eaten, including scorpionfishes which are swallowed head first.

The olive sea snake generally surfaces to breathe at intervals of ten to twenty minutes. It sleeps on the bottom, curled beneath rock or coral. Owing to the slowing down of its body mechanisms it may maintain this position without the need to surface and breathe for many hours. Mainly solitary in its habits, it often becomes gregarious during the mating season. The female produces up to five living young.

The green turtle, *Chelonia mydas*, is very common in some areas along the Great Barrier Reef. Although the beautiful mosaic patterning and colours on young green turtles allow them to be readily identified in the field by a competent observer, smaller specimens are often mistaken for hawksbill turtles. On older green turtles the carapace become a dark blackish-green colour and may be overgrown with weed.

Most breeding grounds are on offshore islands and cays and during the summer months the females go ashore to lay their eggs in the sand above the high-tide line. Several months later the eggs hatch and the young turtles make their way to the water.

The flesh of green turtles makes good eating, the skin makes good leather and other parts have been used in making ornaments and perfumes. The animals have in the past been subject to intensive fishing by humans. Green turtles are now fully protected by law throughout Australia, with the exception of the sustenance fishing carried out by Aborigines.

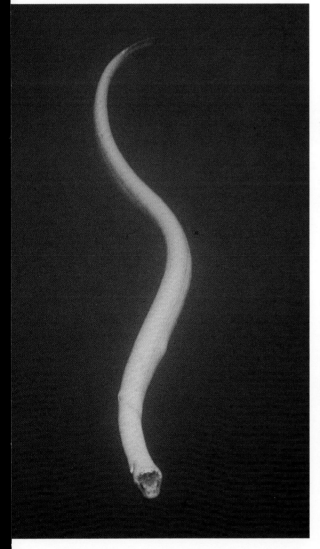

Mammals

The bottlenose dolphin, *Tursiops truncatus*, is an inhabitant of the open ocean and may also be seen in bays, harbours and estuaries.

Dolphins are often referred to as porpoises, but there are no porpoises inhabiting the seas around Australia, just the fourteen species of dolphins. *Tursiops truncatus* may have various shades of grey on the back and may be white on the belly. The short, stout beak has twenty-three to twenty-five pairs of teeth in the jaws and the lower jaw tends to jut out further than the upper.

Dolphins are social mammals and are generally seen in large herds or in smaller family units known as pods. Being mammals, dolphins must breathe air and because of this they swim close to the surface. Food is mainly schooling pelagic fishes which are found by echo-locating. Dolphins are protected throughout Australian waters but many accidental kills occur in shark nets and fishing nets.

Index

Numerals in *italics* denote photographs

Acanthaster planci 14, 15, 26, 46, *46*
Acanthurus lineatus 50, *50*
Acropora sp. 26, *26, 62–3*
Aipysurus laevis 59, *59*
Angas' ovulid (*Phenacovolva angasi*) *6,*
22, *22*
angelfish 24, 54, *54*
Arothron hystrix 46
Arothron nigropunctatus 53, *53*
ascidians 48, *48,* 49, *49*
ass's ear (*Haliotis asinina*) 38, *38*
Asthenosoma intermedium 46, *46*
Aulostoma chinensis 55, *55*

baler shell 38, *38*
banded coral shrimp (*Stenopus hispidus*)
36, *36*
beaked coralfish (*Chelmon rostratus*) 51,
51
black-spotted pufferfish (*Arothron
nigropunctatus*) 53, *53*
blue-lined surgeonfish (*Acanthurus
lineatus*) 50, *50*
blue sea star (*Linckia laevigata*) 47, *47*
blue-stripe squirrelfish (*Sargocentron
tiere*) 52, *52*
bottlenose dolphin (*Tursiops truncatus*)
60, *60*
brain coral, embroidered (*Leptoria
phrygia*) 23, *23*
Bunaster variegatus 49

Calpurnus verrucosus 42, *42*
Caphyra rotundifrons 18
Carapus sp. 44
Caulerpa racemosa 18, *18*
Cephalopholis miniatus 50, *50*
Chaetodontoplus personifer 24
Charonia tritonis 46
Chelmon rostratus 51, *51*
Chelonia mydas 59, *59*
Chlorodesmis comosa 18, *19*
Chromodoris elizabethi 43, *43*
clam, giant fluted (*Tridacna squamosa*) 40,
40
cleaner wrasse, common (*Labroides
dimidiatus*) 52, *52*
cod 12, 50, *50*
Coleman's commensal shrimp
(*Periclimenes colemani*) 46
Comanthina nobilis 44, *44*
Conus textile 42, *42*
Coradion chrysozonus 53, *53*
coral
shield (*Turbinarea peltata*) 22, *22*
staghorn (*Acropora* sp.) 26, *26, 62–3*
sunshine (*Tubastrea aurea*) 16, *16,* 25,
25
Trochel's soft (*Sarcophyton
trocheliophorum*) 27, *27,* 41
coral cod (*Cephalopholis miniatus*) 50, *50*
coral flatworm (*Pseudoceros corallophilus*)
30, *31*
coral shrimp, banded (*Stenopus hispidus*)
36, *36*
coral trout, common (*Plectropoma
leopardus*) 50
coralfish 51, *51,* 53, *53*
cowry
egg (*Ovula ovum*) 41, *41*
map (*Cypraea mappa*) 40, *40*
tiger (*Cypraea tigris*) 39, *39*
toe-nail (*Calpurnus verrucosus*) 42, *42*
crab
depressed gorgonia (*Xenocarcinus
depressus*) 34, *35*
pea (*Pinnotheres* sp.) 38
portunid (*Lissocarcinus polybiodes*) 47
red hermit (*Dardanus megistos*) 32, *32*
splendid reef (*Etisus splendidus*) 33,
33
spotted procellanid (*Petrolisthes
maculatus*) 34, *34*
cray, painted (*Panulirus versicolor*) 37, *37*
crown-of-thorns sea star (*Acanthaster
planci*) 14, 15, 26, 46, *46*
Cymbiolacca pulchra 41, *41*

Cypraea mappa 40, *40*
Cypraea tigris 39, *39*

Dardanus megistos 32, *32*
Dendronephthya 24, 24, 26, *26*
depressed gorgonia crab (*Xenocarcinus
depressus*) 34, *35*
Diadema savignyi 45
Diadema setosum 45, *45*
Didemnum molle 49, *49*
Didemnum moseleyi 49, *49*
distorted ascidian (*Pyctnoclavella detorta*)
48, *48*
dolphin, bottlenose (*Tursiops truncatus*)
60, *60*

egg cowry (*Ovula ovum*) 41, *41*
elegant hydrocoral (*Stylaster elegans*) 25,
25
Elizabeth's chromodoris (*Chromodoris
elizabethi*) 43, *43*
elusive sea urchin (*Asthenosoma
intermedium*) 46, *46*
embroidered brain coral (*Leptoria
phrygia*) 23, *23*
emperor angelfish (*Pomacanthus
imperator*) 54, *54*
Ephinephelus lanceolatus 12, 58, *58*
Epitonium sp. 25
Etisus splendidus 33, *33*

fan sponge, yellow (*Ianthella
flabelliformis*) 20, *20*
feather duster worm (*Spirobranchus
giganteus*) 28, *28*
feather star, noble (*Comanthina nobilis*)
44, *44*
fire fish (*Pterois volitans*) 54, *54*
flatworms 30, *30,* 31
flutemouth, painted (*Aulostoma chinensis*)
55, *55*
four-lined snapper (*Lutjanus kasmira*) 53,
53

Gardiner's notodoris (*Notodoris gardineri*)
21
giant fluted clam (*Tridacna squamosa*) 40,
40
giant triton (*Charonia tritonis*) 46
giant tube worm (*Protula* sp.) 28, *29*
golden ascidian (*Polycarpa aurata*) 48, *48*
golden wentletrap (*Epitonium* sp.) 25
gorgonia crab, depressed (*Xenocarcinus
depressus*) 34, *35*
gorgonian sea fan 17, *17,* 22, 27, *27,* 34
grape weed (*Caulerpa racemosa*) 18, *18*
green turtle (*Chelonia mydas*) 59, *59*
groper, Queensland (*Ephinephelus
lanceolatus*) 12, 58, *58*

Halimeda macroloba 17, *17*
Haliotis asinina 38, *38*
Hancock's flatworm (*Pseudoceros
hancockanus*) 30, *31*
hermit crab, red (*Dardanus megistos*) 32,
32
Heron Island volute (*Cymbiolacca
pulchra*) 41, *41*
Hexabranchus sanguineus 30, 43, *43*
Hiatt's hinge-beak shrimp
(*Rhynchocinetes hiatti*) 32, *32*
horrid stonefish (*Synanceia horrida*) 51,
51
Huenia proteus 17
hussar (*Lutjanus ladetii*) 57, *57*
hydrocoral, elegant (*Stylaster elegans*) 25,
25

Ianthella flabelliformis 20, *20*
icon sea star (*Iconaster longimanus*) 45, *45*
Iconaster longimanus 45, *45*
imperial shrimp (*Periclimenes imperator*)
43, *44*

Labroides dimidiatus 52, *52*
Leptoria phrygia 23, *23*
Linckia laevigata 47, *47*
liparis flatworm (*Pseudoceros liparis*) 30,
30
Lissocarcinus polybiodes 47
Lobophytum pauciflorum 42
Lutjanus kasmira 53, *53*

Lutjanus ladetii 57, *57*
Lutjanus sebae 55, *55*
Lytocarpus philippinus 24, *24*
Lytocarpus phoeniceus 24

Manta alfredi 57, *57*
manta ray (*Manta alfredi*) 57, *57*
map cowry (*Cypraea mappa*) 40, *40*
masked angelfish (*Chaetodontoplus
personifer*) 24
medusa sponge, red 20, *20*
Melithaea sp. 27, *27*
Melo amphora 38, *38*
Moorish idol (*Zanclus cornutus*) 7
Moseley's ascidian (*Didemnum moseleyi*)
49, *49*

nautilus 5, 39, *39*
Nautilus pompilius 5, 39, *39*
noble feather star (*Comanthina nobilis*)
44, *44*
Notodoris gardineri 21

olive sea snake (*Aipsurus laevis*) 59, *59*
orange-banded coralfish (*Coradion
chrysozonus*) 53, *53*
Ovula ovum 41, *41*

painted cray (*Panulirus versicolor*) 37, *37*
painted flutemouth (*Aulostoma chinensis*)
55, *55*
Panulirus versicolor 37, *37*
paper nautilus 39
pea (*Pinnotheres* sp.) 38
pearl fish, slimbodied (*Carapus* sp.) 44
pearly nautilus (*Nautilus pompilius*) 5,
39, *39*
Pediculariona stylasteris 25
Pellasimnia semperi 27
Pentaceraster regulus 47, *47*
Pericharax heteroaphis 21, *21*
Periclimenes colemani 46
Periclimenes imperator 43, *44*
Periclimenes soror 46
Petrolisthes maculatus 34, *34*
Phenacovolva angasi *6,* 22, *22*
Phestilla melanobranchia 25
Pinnotheres sp. 38
Plectropoma leopardus 50
Polycarpa aurata 48, *48*
Pomacanthus imperator 54, *54*
portunid crab (*Lissocarcinus polybiodes*)
47
princely sea star (*Pentaceraster regulus*)
47, *47*
procellanid crab, spotted (*Petrolisthes
maculatus*) 34, *34*
Protula sp. 28, *29* .
Pseudoceros corallophilus 30, *31*
Pseudoceros hancockanus 30, *31*
Pseudoceros liparis 30, *30*
Pterois volitans 54, *54*
pufferfish 46, 53, *53*
Pyctnoclavella detorta 48, *48*

Queensland groper (*Ephinephelus
lanceolatus*) 12, 58, *58*

ray, manta (*Manta alfredi*) 57, *57*
red and white sea fan (*Melithaea* sp.) 27,
27
red emperor (*Lutjanus sebae*) 55, *55*
red hermit crab (*Dardanus megistos*) 32,
32
red medusa sponge 20, *20*
red sea fan (*Melithaea* sp.) 27
reef crab, splendid (*Etisus splendidus*) 33,
33
reef shark, white-tipped (*Triaenodon
obesus*) 56, *56*
Rhynchocinetes hiatti 32, *32*

Sarcophyton trocheliophorum 27, *27,* 41
Sargocentron tiere 52, *52*
sea cucumber, variegated (*Stichopus
variegatus*) 44, *44*
sea fan 17, *17,* 22, 23, *23,* 27, *27,* 34
sea fern, white stinging (*Lytocarpus
philippinus*) 24, *24*
sea snake, olive (*Aipsurus laevis*) 59, *59*
sea star 14, 15, 26, 45, *45,* 46, 46, 47, *47*
sea urchin 45, *45,* 46, *46*

shark, white-tipped reef (*Triaenodon
obesus*) 56, *56*
shield coral (*Turbinarea peltata*) 22, *22*
shrimp
banded coral (*Stenopus hispidus*) 36,
36
Coleman's commensal (*Periclimenes
colemani*) 46
Hiatt's hinge-beak (*Rhynchocinetes
hiatti*) 32, *32*
imperial (*Periclimenes imperator*) 43,
44
Stimpson's snapping (*Synalpheus
stimpsoni*) 36, *36*
Siphonogorgia sp. 23, *23*
slimbodied pearl fish (*Carapus* sp.) 44
snapper, four-lined (*Lutjanus kasmira*)
53, *53*
soft coral sea fan (*Siphonogorgia* sp.) 23,
23
soft didemnum (*Didemnum molle*) 49, *49*
Spanish dancer nudibranch
(*Hexabranchus sanguineus*) 30, 43, *43*
spiny sea urchin (*Diadema setosum*) 45,
45
Spirobranchus giganteus 28, *28*
splendid reef crab (*Etisus splendidus*) 33,
33
sponge 20, *20,* 21, *21*
spotted procellanid crab (*Petrolisthes
maculatus*) 34, *34*
squirrelfish, blue-stripe (*Sargocentron
tiere*) 52, *52*
staghorn coral (*Acropora* sp.) 26, *26, 62–3*
Stenopus hispidus 36, *36*
Stitchopus variegatus 44, *44*
Stimpson's snapping shrimp (*Synalpheus
stimpsoni*) 36, *36*
stonefish, horrid (*Synanceia horrida*) 51,
51
Stylaster elegans 25, *25*
sunshine coral (*Tubastrea aurea*) 16, *16,*
25, *25*
surgeonfish, blue-lined (*Acanthurus
lineatus*) 50, *50*
Synalpheus stimpsoni 36, *36*
Synanceia horrida 51, *51*

textile cone (*Conus textile*) 42, *42*
Thalassoma lutescens 56, *56*
tiger cowry (*Cypraea tigris*) 39, *39*
toe-nail cowry (*Calpurnus verrucosus*) 42,
42
Triaenodon obesus 56, *56*
Tridacna squamosa 40, *40*
triton, giant (*Charonia tritonis*) 46
Trochel's soft coral (*Sarcophyton
trocheliophorum*) 27, *27,* 41
trout, common coral (*Plectropoma
leopardus*) 50
Tubastrea aurea 16, *16,* 25, *25*
tube worm, giant (*Protula* sp.) 28, *29*
Turbinarea peltata 22, *22*
Tursiops truncatus 60, *60*
turtle, green (*Chelonia mydas*) 59, *59*
turtle weed (*Chlorodesmis comosa*) 18, *19*

variegated sea cucumber (*Stichopus
variegatus*) 44, *44*
volcano sponge (*Pericharax heteroaphis*)
21, *21*
volute, Heron Island (*Cymbiolacca
pulchra*) 41, *41*

wentletrap, golden (*Epitonium* sp.) 25
white stinging sea fern (*Lytocarpus
philippinus*) 24, *24*
white-tipped reef shark (*Triaenodon
obesus*) 56, *56*
wrasses 52, *52,* 56, *56*

Xenocarcinus depressus 34, *35*

yellow fan sponge (*Ianthella flabelliformis*)
20, *20*
yellow-green wrasse (*Thalassoma
lutescens*) 56, *56*

Zanclus cornutus 7
Zenopontia noverca 47